First Facts®

Christmas around the World

Christmas in
ITALY

by Jack Manning

CAPSTONE PRESS
a capstone imprint

First Facts are published by Capstone Press,
1710 Roe Crest Drive, North Mankato, Minnesota 56003
www.capstonepub.com

Library of Congress Cataloging-in-Publication Data
Manning, Jack.
Christmas in Italy / by Jack Manning.
    pages cm.—(First facts: Christmas around the world)
Includes index.
ISBN 978-1-4765-3100-7 (library binding)
ISBN 978-1-4765-3431-2 (ebook PDF)
1. Christmas—Italy—Juvenile literature. 2. Italy—Social life and customs—Juvenile literature.
I. Title.
GT4987.51.M36 2014
394.26630945—dc23   2013003953

Editorial Credits
Brenda Haugen, editor; Gene Bentdahl, designer; Eric Gohl, media researcher;
Kathy McColley, production specialist

Photo Credits
BigStockPhoto.com: agno_agnus, 11; Capstone Studio: Karon Dubke, 9, 21; Dreamstime:
Antoniogravante, 5; Fotolia: jovannig, 17; Getty Images: Franco Origlia, cover; Newscom: EPA/
Claudio Onorati, 14, Getty Images/AFP/Filippo Monteforte, 20; Shutterstock: Angelo Giampiccolo,
13, Francesco Dazzi, 6, Marco Mayer, 18, Pasquale Lazzaro, 1

Design Elements: Shutterstock

Printed in China by Nordica.
0413/CA21300423
032013   007226NORDF13

TABLE OF CONTENTS

Christmas in 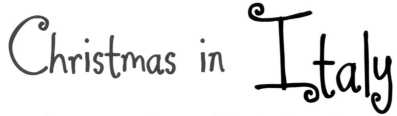 Italy

Strings of sparkly lights hang along city streets. Delicious smells of chicken and pasta drift from homes. Joyful music rises from markets. It must be Christmas in Italy!

People in Italy celebrate Christmas Day on December 25. But the season of Christmas lasts much longer. It begins eight days before Christmas Day. The Christmas season ends after Epiphany, which is January 6.

How to Say It!
In Italy people say *"Buon Natale"* (BWON nah-TAWL-ee), which means "Good Christmas."

CHRISTMAS FACT!

A bright star led the *tre re magi* (TRAY RAY MAH-jee) to the baby Jesus. Tre re magi means "three wise kings" in Italian. The three men brought Jesus gifts.

The First Christmas

Christmas is a **Christian** holiday celebrating the birth of **Jesus**. Mary and Joseph were Jesus' parents. Long ago Mary and Joseph traveled to the Middle Eastern city of Bethlehem. The couple did not have a place to stay. They spent the night in a stable. Jesus was born in the stable.

Christian—a person who follows a religion based on the teachings of Jesus
Jesus—the founder of the Christian religion

Christmas Celebrations

Shepherds also visited baby Jesus in the stable. Children in Italy dress as shepherds on December 23. They do this to remember the shepherds at the first Christmas.

Children act out the Christmas story in school. Some dress as Mary and Joseph. Others dress as angels or shepherds.

Most families open gifts on Christmas Day. Some families also open gifts on Epiphany. On Epiphany people remember the gifts the three kings gave Jesus.

Buon Natale!

Christmas Symbols

In the Bethlehem stable, Jesus slept in a **manger**. A special Christmas symbol in Italy is the manger, called the *presepio* (pre-ZEP-ee-oh).

Most people put figures of Mary and Joseph in presepios. Some also hold angels and the three kings. People may place sheep, oxen, and donkey figures in the presepios too. They add Jesus on Christmas Eve.

manger—a food box for animals

CHRISTMAS FACT!

People display presepios in churches, homes, or outdoors. Some people pray or sing to the mangers to honor Jesus. Some place presents for Jesus in front of presepios.

Christmas Decorations

People hang many kinds of **ornaments** from their Christmas trees. Angels, stars, and glass balls are popular ornaments.

Children hang stockings over fireplaces or doors or on walls. They find gifts in the stockings on Epiphany.

People also decorate their towns for the Christmas season. They hang strings of lights along the streets. Some put lights on shop windows.

ornament—a decoration hung on a Christmas tree

CHRISTMAS FACT!

Many children believe Befana stops at every house where a child lives. She wants to see if the young person is Jesus. She leaves a gift for each child.

14

Santa Claus

Some children wait for Father Christmas, who is called Babbo Natale (BAH-boh nah-TAWL-ee). He brings gifts on Christmas Day.

Many children also look for a kind old witch named Befana (bay-FAH-nah). People believe the three kings invited Befana to Bethlehem to honor Jesus. She said she was too busy. Later she changed her mind. But she did not find the baby Jesus. Many children believe Befana still looks for Jesus every Epiphany.

Christmas Presents

Pretty gifts wrapped in shiny paper lie under the Christmas trees. Children open the presents on Christmas Day.

Many children get gifts from Babbo Natale and Befana. They open gifts from Babbo Natale on Christmas Day. They unwrap presents from Befana on Epiphany. Children usually receive toys as gifts.

Many Italians give panettone (pan-eh-TOHN-eh) as gifts. It is a bread with raisins and candied fruit.

Christmas Food

People enjoy many **traditional** foods during the Christmas season. Some Italians eat chicken and stuffing on Christmas Day. Others eat baked eel or pasta.

Most families eat lentils on New Year's Day. They believe these beans are symbols of money. They hope eating lentils will bring them more money in the new year.

traditional—handed down from one generation to another within a family or culture

Christmas Songs

Music is often heard in markets during the Christmas season. Many musicians play in the markets while shoppers buy gifts and food.

Italy is famous for its bagpipers, who are called *zampognari* (dsahm-pahn-YAR-ee). These musicians are mountain shepherds who come to cities each Christmas. They stop at outdoor presepios and play music to show respect for Jesus.

CHRISTMAS FACT!

Some people believe that zampognari played for Jesus' mother, Mary.

Hands-On:
MAKE A DECORATED ORNAMENT

Ornaments are popular Christmas decorations in Italy. You can make your own fancy ornament to brighten your home.

What You Need

- paper and pencil
- newspaper
- clear plastic ornament
- tempera paints
- small paintbrushes

What You Do

1. Practice one or two designs with your paper and pencil before you begin to paint. You may want to draw a Christmas tree or a star. Or you may want to draw your own design.
2. Prepare your work space by spreading newspaper over the area. Wash and dry your ornament before you start painting.
3. Hold the ornament in one hand. Use a brush to paint your design on one side of the ornament. Let the paint dry.
4. Paint the other side of the ornament. Let the paint dry.
5. Hang the ornament for everyone to enjoy.

GLOSSARY

Christian (KRIS-chuhn)—a person who follows a religion based on the teachings of Jesus

Jesus (JEE-zuhss)—the founder of the Christian religion

manger (MAYN-jur)—a food box for animals

ornament (OR-nuh-muhnt)—a decoration hung on a Christmas tree

traditional (truh-DISH-uh-nul)—handed down from one generation to another within a family or culture

READ MORE

Donaldson, Madeline. *Italy.* Country Explorers.
Minneapolis: Lerner, 2011.

Kalz, Jill. *My First Italian Phrases.* Speak Another Language!
North Mankato, Minn.: Picture Window Books, 2013.

Throp, Claire. *Italy.* Countries Around the World.
Chicago: Heinemann Library, 2012.

INTERNET SITES

FactHound offers a safe, fun way to find Internet sites related
to this book. All of the sites on FactHound have been researched
by our staff.

Here's all you do:

Visit *www.facthound.com*

Type in this code: 9781476531007

INDEX